Contents

What is a habitat?

A **habitat** is a place where plants and animals can get what they need to live. What do they need? Like you, they need food, water, and shelter.

woodpecker

HORRIBLE HABITATS
The Compost Heap

Sharon Katz Cooper

www.raintreepublishers.co.uk
Visit our website to find out more information about Raintree books.

To order:
☎ Phone 0845 6044371
🖨 Fax +44 (0) 1865 312263
💻 Email myorders@raintreepublishers.co.uk

Customers from outside the UK please telephone +44 1865 312262

Raintree is an imprint of Capstone Global Library Limited, a company incorporated in England and Wales having its registered office at 7 Pilgrim Street, London, EC4V 6LB – Registered company number: 6695582

Text © Capstone Global Library Limited 2010
First published in hardback in 2010
Paperback edition first published in 2011

Edited by Charlotte Guillain, Rebecca Rissman, and Siân Smith
Designed by Joanna Hinton-Malivoire
Picture research by Tracy Cummins and Heather Mauldin
Originated by Chroma Graphics (Overseas) Pte. Ltd
Printed and bound in China by Leo Paper Products

ISBN 978 1 406212 93 8 (hardback)
14 13 12 11 10
10 9 8 7 6 5 4 3 2 1

ISBN 978 1 406213 01 0 (paperback)
14 13 12 11 10
10 9 8 7 6 5 4 3 2 1

British Library Cataloguing in Publication Data
Katz Cooper, Sharon.
The compost heap. -- (Horrible habitats)
577.5'54-dc22
A full catalogue record for this book is available from the British Library.

Acknowledgements
The author and publisher are grateful to the following for permission to reproduce copyright material: Age Fotostock p. **29** (© ARCO/J Meul); Alamy pp. **7** (© Kathy deWitt), **10** (© Mark Boulton), **12** (© Mediacolors), **15** (© Graham Corney), **19** (© David Chapman); Ardea pp. **22** (© John Mason), **23** (© Mark Boulton); Dwight Kuhn Photography p. **24** (© Dwight Kuhn); Getty Images pp. **5** (© Roine Magnusson), **6** (© Xavier Bonghi), **18** (© DEA/Christian Ricci); Minden p. **25** (© Mitsuhiko Imamori); National Geographic Stock p. **27** (© Kim Wolhuter); Photolibrary pp. **9** (© Andrea Jones), **20** (Bildagentur RM); Photoresearchers, Inc. pp. **13** (© SciMAT), **16** (© SPL); Photoshot p. **14** (© Bruce Coleman Inc/Bartomeu Borrell); Shutterstock pp. **4** (© Steve Byland), **8** (© Colour), **11** (© Shutterlist), **21** (© ENOXH), **26** (© Dr. Morley Read); Visuals Unlimited, Inc. p. **17** (© Nigel Cattlin).

Cover photograph of kitchen waste reproduced with permission of Photoresearchers, Inc. (© Mark Boulton).

Every effort has been made to contact copyright holders of material reproduced in this book. Any omissions will be rectified in subsequent printings if notice is given to the publishers.

Some words are shown in bold, **like this**. You can find out what they mean by looking in the glossary.

rotting food

Did you know your leftover food could be used again? A compost heap is a pile of rotting food. This pile of rotting food is a **habitat** too!

A compost heap is made of fruit and vegetable scraps. You might also find old newspapers, leaves, and dead plants there. They are all slowly rotting. The living things in the compost heap turn it all into fresh soil!

This mouldy banana is slowly rotting.

Compost heaps must be dark, warm, and a little bit wet. That is the best **habitat** for the animals and tiny living things who turn the food scraps into soil. The tiny living things are called **microbes**.

compost heap

eggshell

tea bag

banana peel

11

These apples are starting
to rot, or break down.

12

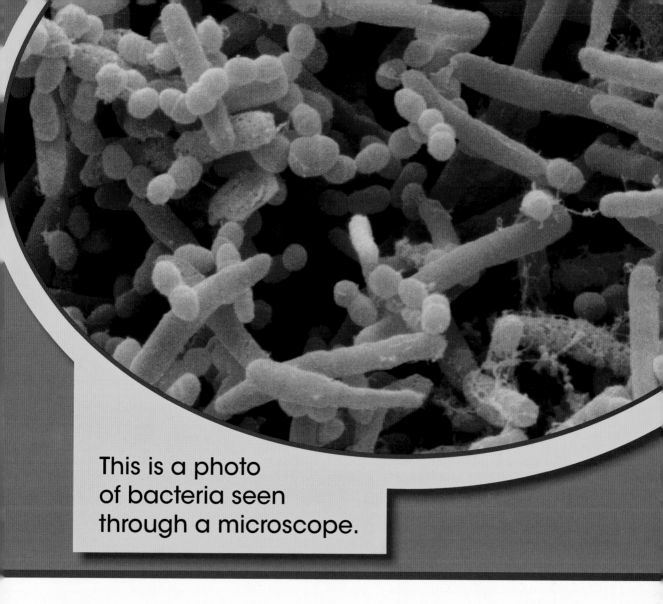

This is a photo
of bacteria seen
through a microscope.

Bacteria are **microbes.** They are so
small you can only see them through
a microscope. **Fungi** are also microbes.
Bacteria and fungi get to work first.
They begin breaking down food
scraps into smaller pieces.

Here come the worms!

Worms are the superstars of a compost **habitat**! You can find worms in many compost heaps. They eat the rotting food. Then the worms poo out rich soil.

FUN FACT

If a worm's skin dries out it will die because a worm breathes through its skin.

15

Worms have many **segments**, or parts. Some of the segments have tiny stiff hairs. Worms use these hairs to help them move.

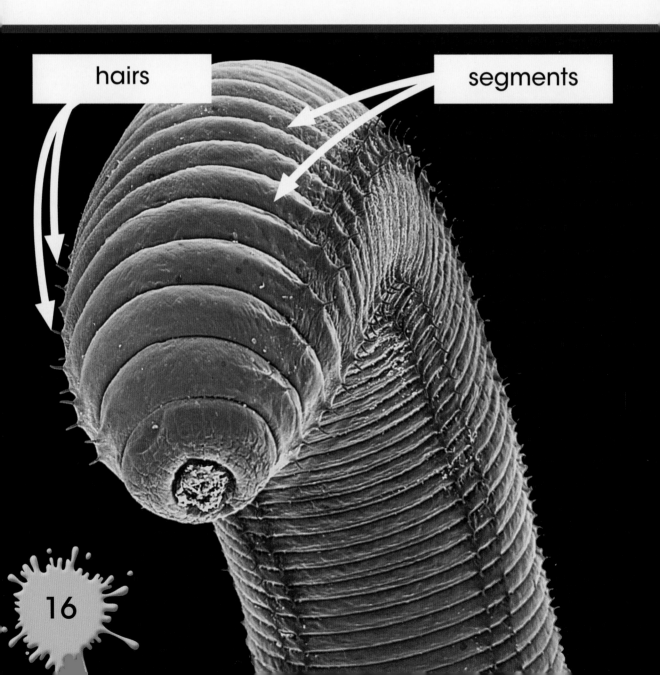

hairs

segments

Except for those hairs, worms have nothing else sticking out from their bodies. This long, smooth shape helps them **burrow** or dig down into the compost.

mucus

Worms make a lot of slippery **mucus** on their skins. Mucus covers their bodies. It keeps them wet and helps them to slide through food scraps and soil.

FUN FACT

Worms have no eyes but can still sense light and will move away from it.

19

Squirming and sucking

Compost worms squirm through food scraps. They suck up rotting food. Strong muscles in the worms' gut mix up food with **digestive juices**. This breaks down the food into smaller and smaller bits.

These worms are busy eating rotting food.

Worms poo out little piles of partly digested food. Believe it or not, these piles make great soil. It is perfect as **fertilizer**, which is something used to help plants grow.

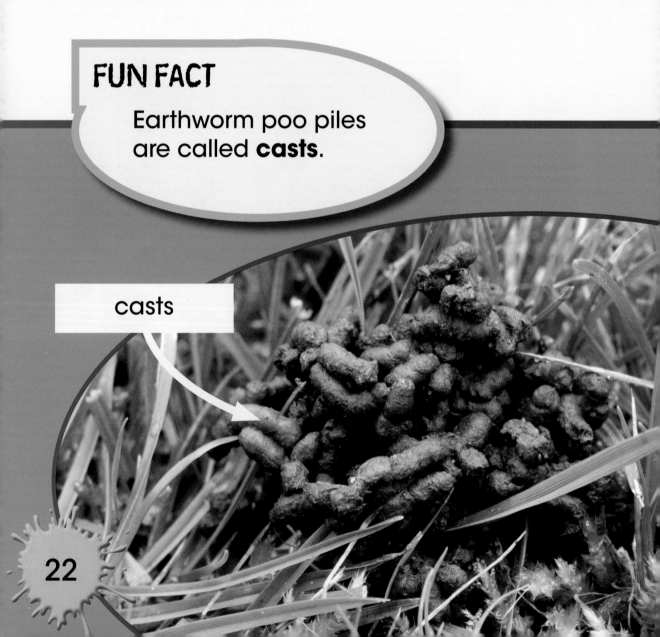

casts

22

Earthworm poo is rich in **nutrients**.
Nutrients are things plants need
to help them grow.

Woodlouse poo

Worms are not the only animals in the compost heap. There are also lots of woodlice. These little creatures chew up dead plants. They leave behind little pellets of poo. The pellets are full of **nutrients** for good soil.

woodlouse

woodlouse poo

25

Vomiting flies

Flies also like to feed on rotting fruits and vegetables. They vomit on their food before they eat it. The vomit helps to break down the food. Then they can slurp it up with their tongues.

Watch a worm

What you need:
- a place with earthworms
- gardening gloves (if you'd like to use these)
- your eyes

What to do:
1. Find a good outdoor place with soil and earthworms in it.

2. Dig around a little bit with your hands to break up the soil. Dig until you bring up some worms.

3. Choose one or two worms and watch them for a while.

4. What do you see them do? How do they move? Do you see them eating? How do they do it?

Glossary

bacteria type of tiny living thing you can see only through a microscope

burrow to dig in

casts piles of worm poo

digestive juices liquids in the stomach that help break down food

fertilizer something that helps make soil better for growing things in

fungi plant-like living things like mushrooms

habitat place where animals or plants live and grow

microbes tiny living things you can see only through a microscope

mucus slippery slime produced by some animals. Humans make mucus too.

nutrients something that plants and animals need to stay healthy and grow

segment section or part

Find out more

Find out

How many hearts does a worm have?

Books to read

Let's-Read-and-Find-Out Science: Wiggling Worms at Work, Wendy Pfeffer (HarperCollins Publishers, 2004)

The Amazing World of Microlife: Microlife that Rots Things, Steve Parker (Raintree, 2006)

Where to Find Minibeasts: Minibeasts in the Compost Heap, Sarah Ridley (Franklin Watts, 2009)

Websites

http://news.bbc.co.uk/cbbcnews/hi/newsid_8030000/newsid_8032800/8032803.stm
Watch the video on this website to learn how some kids made a compost heap on a roof!

http://www.opalexplorenature.org?q=KidsZone
Make you own wormery – this website tells you how.

http://yucky.discovery.com/flash/worm/pg000102.html
You can learn all about worms on this website.

Index